CAN YOU SOLVE THESE?

Mathematical problems to
test your thinking powers
SERIES No. 2

DAVID WELLS

TARQUIN PUBLICATIONS

THE PROBLEM SOLVER

Most of the problems in this book first appeared, sometimes in a different form, in issues 4, 5 and 6 of The Problem Solver, written and edited by David Wells and published by Rain Publications, 6 Carmarthen Road, Westbury-on-Trym, Bristol, England.

Our thanks are due to the boys of the Royal Hospital School, Holbrook. In the true spirit of enthusiastic problem solving, they showed us how several of our original solutions could be improved.

0 906212 34 0
© DAVID WELLS 1984
EDITED BY JEAN SLACK
DESIGN WILSON SMITH
PRINTED BY
THE FIVE CASTLES PRESS LTD. IPSWICH

TARQUIN PUBLICATIONS
STRADBROKE
DISS
NORFOLK IP21 5JP

PROBLEM SOLVING

All the problems in this book are based on mathematical ideas and mathematical thinking, but don't worry if you have forgotten most of the mathematics you ever knew. Common-sense and ingenuity, perseverence and a flash of insight will be more useful than book-knowledge. Some of these problems are easy, some are difficult, but they have been chosen for your enjoyment. Problem solving is fun!

If you get really stuck there is a HINTS section which offers help without giving away the solution. For the truly desperate there is also a SOLUTIONS section which is printed upside-down to act as a discouragement. Often the solution itself suggests another problem which would be interesting to investigate and we hope these will be used as a starting point for problems and investigations of your own.

This second collection of problems also includes some which are interesting to solve using a micro or a programmable calculator. However, they may also be solved by traditional methods too and access to a machine is not essential. Such questions are marked with an 'M'

Good problem solving!

David Wells

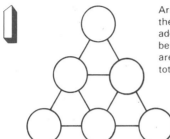

1 Arrange the numbers 1 to 6 in these circles, so that when you add up all the differences between pairs of circles which are next to each other, your total is as large as possible.

Given that
$13^2 = 169$ $133^2 = 17689$ $1333^2 = 1776889$
and
$16^2 = 256$ $166^2 = 27556$ $1666^2 = 2775556$

Without using a calculator or a computer can you write down the answers to

$13333^2 =$ $16666^2 =$

Can you find another number between 10 and 20 which, if you keep repeating the second digit, and squaring, has the same number pattern?

3 If p and q are two numbers between 0 and 1, then p+q—pq will also be a number between 0 and 1. Why?

5

This is a game of three-dimensional noughts and crosses.

Imagine that the boards are one above the other in a vertical pile.

You can only win by getting a line of four in any direction.

(That includes those diagonal and vertical lines which go through all four layers from top to bottom).

It is 'crosses' turn to play. What is 'crosses' best move?

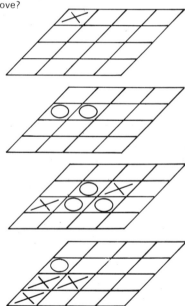

5

I think of a positive number, add one, multiply my answer by itself, take away twice the number I first thought of, and my answer is 26. What number did I think of?

6

Two points are on opposite sides of a straight line. Is it true that you can always find a point on the line which is the same distance from each of the two points, whatever their positions?

7

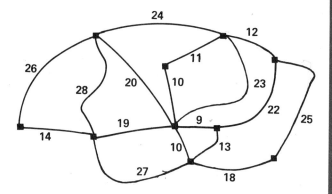

A travelling salesman is planning his weekly trip to all of the towns on this map. On each trip he must visit each town at least once, starting and finishing at the same town, which he can choose.

Naturally he wants to make his trip as short as he can. Which town would you advise him to start in, and which route should he follow?

Fit these numbers into this
cross-number diagram:

125	335	272	247
299	718	904	739
48	43	40	12	32
15	53	39	62	63
33	41	21	90	79
69	25	11	16	77

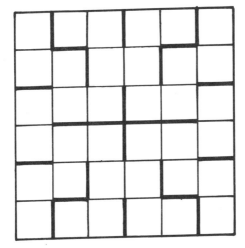

Two of these expressions always have the same value,
whatever number you choose N to be. Which two are they?

$N^2 - 1$ $7N + 5$ $(N+1)(N-2)$

$2N^2 + N$ $N^2 - N - 2$

9

This BUSH has 4 flowers and 2 joints, making 6 flowers and joints in total.

(The point where the root goes into the ground does not count as a joint in this problem).

How many bushes can you find with a total of 6 joints and flowers?

Each stem must end with a flower. Do not bother about the order of the branches or whether they grow to the left or the right.

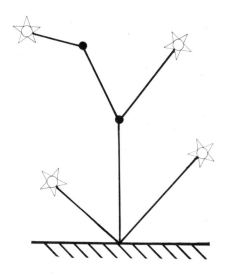

11

What fraction, when you turn it into a decimal, starts like this:
0.0204081632 . . . .?

What fraction, when you turn it into a decimal, starts like this:
0.0103092781 . . . .?

12

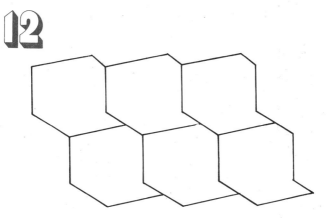

This is a tessellation of identical 7-sided polygons. Can you
design a tessellation of identical 9-sided polygons?

13

The diagram shows an irregular tetrahedron, or triangular pyramid.

Is it possible to construct an irregular tetrahedron whose six edges are 4, 5, 6, 7, 8 and 9 cms long?

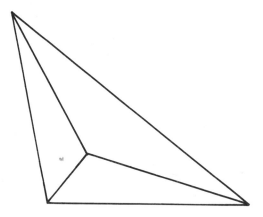

Find 6 numbers, such that with six straight line segments of those lengths, it is impossible to construct a tetrahedron.

14

Find the *exact* value of sin 10° x sin 50° x sin 70°. (Tables will not be of any use).

15 ^M

Find the sums of these series:

$\frac{1}{2} + \frac{2}{4} + \frac{3}{8} + \frac{4}{16} + \frac{5}{32} + \ldots$

$\frac{1}{2} + \frac{3}{4} + \frac{5}{8} + \frac{7}{16} + \frac{9}{32} + \ldots$

16

Complete this table for an
eight-player all-play-all tennis
tournament, by marking in each
cell the round in which the
players along the top and down
the side will play.

	A	B	C	D	E	F	G	H
A	✕							
B		✕						
C			✕					
D				✕				
E					✕			
F						✕		
G							✕	
H								✕

17

This diagram shows two points P and Q moving along two straight lines. Each point moves at a steady speed but their speeds may not be the same.

The points S and T also move, so that PQST is always a square.

What paths do S and T follow?

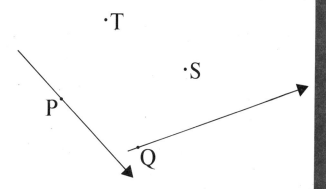

18

Here are two sequences of numbers. If each sequence goes on for ever, which sequence has the most numbers in it?

(A) 1 2 3 4 5 6 7 8 9 10 11 12 13 14 . . .
(B) 1 4 9 16 25 36 49 64 81 100 121 144 . .

19 Can eight points be marked on a piece of paper, so that it is *not* possible to draw a convex pentagon by joining five of them with straight lines?

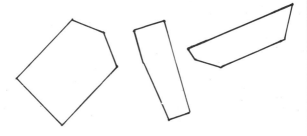

20

This cone has a slant height of 30cm and the radius of the base is 10cm.

Point A is on the base and point B is exactly opposite but two-thirds of the way up the side.

Find the shortest distance from A to B, along the surface of the cone.

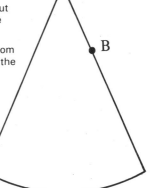

21

Find as many pairs of positive numbers as you can which fit this equation:

$$2p + 3q = 25$$

Investigate patterns between these number pairs.

22

Six new towns have to be joined by roads so that it is possible to travel from one town to any other town in only one way. (You are allowed to travel through a town to get to another).

The roads do not meet or cross each other, except at one of the towns. What is the smallest number of new roads needed? What is the largest number of new roads that could be used?

23

Prove that the pentagon is more than twice the area of the pentagram star by dissecting the pentagon into several pieces which will make two of the stars, with a bit left over.

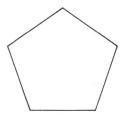 

24

Two proof readers are checking the same manuscript. The first reader spots 84 errors and the second spots 72. These figures include 60 mistakes which are spotted by both proof readers.

How many errors would you estimate there are in the manuscript in total?

25

Which of these statements are true?
'One fifth is the average of one fourth and one sixth.'
'One third exceeds a quarter by one third of a quarter.'
'One third of one fifth is greater than one fifth of one third.'

26

A	G	H	J	K	L
B					
C					
D					
E					
F					

Across clues:
A: Factor of 999,999
B: 5 times A across
C: B across — A across
D: B across + A across
E: D across — C across
F: A across + E across

Down clues:
A: Multiple of 176
G: Same multiple of 418
H: G down — A down
J: 999,999 — A down
K: 999,999 — G down
L: 999,999 — H down

27

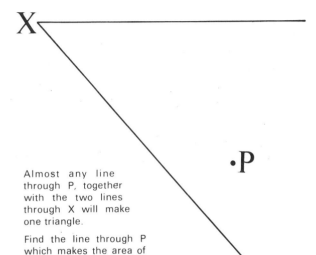

Almost any line through P, together with the two lines through X will make one triangle.

Find the line through P which makes the area of this triangle as small as possible.

28 ^M

Exactly 63.41463414% of the people asked if they used 'Scrubbo' soap powder, replied 'Yes'.

What is the smallest number of people who could have been asked the question?

Each of these true statements refers to seven out of eight of the living members of the Jones and King families, either by their personal name or by their relationship to another member.

John's wife's sister's husband's mother's son is Peter's cousin's father.

Sally's grandaughter's cousin's father's sister-in-law is Gregory's son-in-law's wife.

If Anita has no children, what relationship is she to Mike?

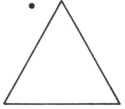

How big is the largest equilateral triangle that can be drawn on squared dotted paper so that not even one dot is inside the triangle or on any of its edges?

31

Here are three sections, (the kind you would get by cutting in one direction with a flat knife), of a well-known solid:

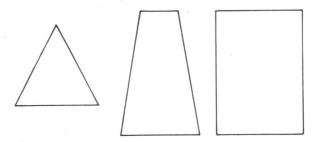

What shape might it be?

32

Find a fraction which is greater than $\frac{7}{17}$ but less than $\frac{5}{12}$.

Draw any triangle and then try to find three points, A, B and C, one on each side of the triangle, (but not at the corners), so that the area of triangle ABC is one half of the area of the original triangle.

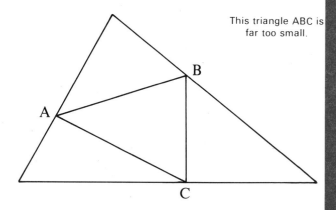

This triangle ABC is far too small.

Is it possible to find three numbers, called A, B and C, such that: A + B = 13, B + C = 15 and C = A + 1?

A pill for a certain illness must not be taken more than once in any period of an hour, or more than 6 in any period of 12 hours.

What is the largest number of pills which could be safely taken in 18 hours?

This drawing shows a knot in a continuous loop of rope. Rearrange the knot, without cutting the rope, to make it as symmetrical as possible.

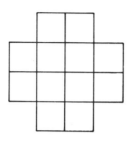
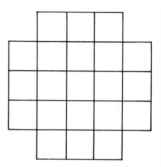

To tackle this problem you need to know the knight's move in chess. Choose any square to start with, then move to another square a knight's move away. Go on moving like a knight until you have moved to as many squares as possible, *once each*.

What is the largest number of squares that is visited, in each case?

$$\frac{1}{2} - (\frac{1}{3} + \frac{1}{9} + \frac{1}{27} + \ldots)$$
$$= \frac{1}{2} - \frac{1}{3} - (\frac{1}{9} + \frac{1}{27} + \ldots)$$
$$= \frac{1}{6} - (\frac{1}{9} + \frac{1}{27} + \ldots)$$

Therefore . . .? Complete this argument.

Using a theodolite, a surveyor measures the bearings of several landmarks. He then moves 50 metres North and measures the bearings of the same objects again. Does he have enough information to draw a map of the landmarks?

Suppose that he had taken the bearings of the same landmarks from three separate positions, but without knowing any of the distances between these positions. Would he have enough information to draw a map of them?

The distances of a point T from the corners of an equilateral triangle are 3, 5 and 7cms. What is the size of the equilateral triangle?

41

Here is a circle. How could you discover exactly the position of its centre by using only a pair of compasses and a straight edge?

(A straight edge is a ruler which you are not allowed to mark and which is not marked in any way to start with).

42

In The Daily Gush poll of sports correspondents to find the Sports Personality of the year, Ian Botham came first with 15 votes, Sebastian Coe came second with 8 votes and Steve Davis came third with 4 votes.

The Morning Spout asked exactly the same sports correspondents to vote for their Sports Star 1981 and got these results: Botham 87 points, Sebastian Coe 76 points and Steve Davis 65 points.

Is there a contradiction here?

M

Investigate the different values of this expression, if t is any number between 0 and 5. What is its greatest value?

$$50t - 35t^2 + 10t^3 - t^4$$

44

This diagram shows how the pages of any 16 page booklet must be arranged before printing so that when each large sheet is folded, stapled and then trimmed, the pages will appear the right way up in their correct order.

Curiously, the sum of the page numbers is always 34 horizontally. Can you rearrange them slightly so that the verticals and diagonals also make 34? (in other words make it into a 4 x 4 magic square).

FRONT

1	16	13	4
8	9	12	5

BACK

3	14	15	2
6	11	10	7

What is the volume of the largest rectangular block that can be rotated in any direction inside a rectangular box whose inside measurements are 20 x 15 x 10 cm?

This is a game for two players. To start, mark some points on a piece of paper, like this.

One player plays first and at each turn the player joins two of the points with a straight line. It is forbidden to draw a line which crosses another line or to draw more than one line through a point. The last player to draw a line is the winner.

In a 5 x 5 Latin Square each of the same five symbols appears once in each row and once in each column.

Is it possible to complete this Latin Square by adding two more of each symbol in the empty lines?

Is it always possible to complete a Latin Square, if the rows and columns already marked do not repeat any of the symbols?

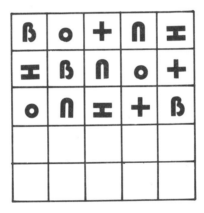

Alan and Mary's ages add up to 25. Mary and Gary's add up to 29.

Caroline is 14. Her age is exactly half way between Alan and Gary's ages. How old is everyone?

49

Explain why every prime number, with two exceptions, must be one more or one less than a multiple of 6.

50

Choose three directions, like this:

Then draw a circle, choose a point on it to start from, and set off in the first direction. Change to the second direction when you meet the edge... change to the third direction... back to the first direction, and so on.

What happens if you continue?

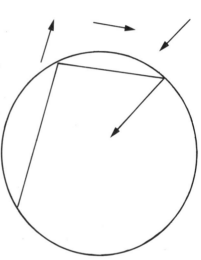

51

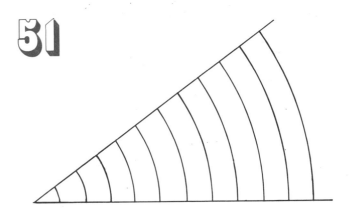

Are there any pairs of areas in this figure, such that one area is three times the area of the other? (The curved lines are all parts of circles, and the distance between each curved line and the next is the same).

52 ^M

How many terms of this series:

$$\tfrac{1}{2} + \tfrac{1}{3} + \tfrac{1}{4} + \tfrac{1}{5} + \tfrac{1}{6} + \dots$$

are needed to make the sum of the series greater than $2\tfrac{1}{2}$?

In each of these two problems you are told how much each row and each column adds up to. You have to discover what numbers should go in the squares.

How many different solutions does each problem have?

Can you invent a problem of the same kind which has only *one* solution?

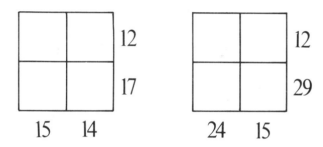

In each of these two problems you are told how much each row and each column adds up to. You have to discover what numbers should go in the squares.

How many different solutions does each problem have?

If these seven points were marked on a graph in the usual way, five of them would lie on a straight line. *Without* drawing a graph, can you pick out the two points which would *not* lie on that line?

(9, 17) (6, 11) (3, 5) (7, 12) (3½, 6) (5, 10) (5, 9)

How could you divide this rectangle into 24 equal parts, as accurately as possible, without using a ruler to measure anything or to draw straight lines?

56

What is the difference between '999999 thousand' and 999899001?

57

In our local bank, every customer joins the same queue and the person at the front of the queue moves to the first cashier to become available.

In any period of 1 minute, (for example from 2.37 to 2.38) there is a 1 in 2 chance that one person will enter the bank, 1 in 4 that two people will enter, 1 in 8 that three will enter and so on.

On average it takes 2 minutes to serve one customer.

Investigate the length of the queue during the day and the number of cashiers needed.

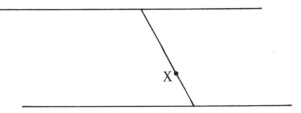

The horizontal lines in this figure are parallel. The line through X between the parallel lines is divided by X in the ratio 2 to 1. (That means that one part is twice the other).
Is it possible to draw a straight line through X between the parallel lines which is *not* divided in the ratio 2 to 1?

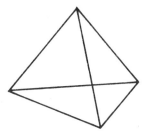

Can a regular tetrahedron made of hard rubber be used as a plug for a square hole of suitable size?

60

In this map the shaded area is desert which can only be crossed at 15 kph. The unshaded area is grassland which can be crossed at 60 kph. How should E.X. Plorer get from A to Z as quickly as possible?

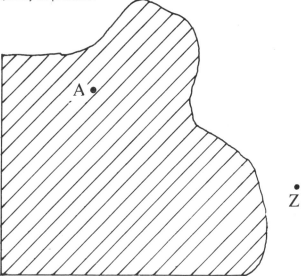

61

You have two straight lengths of wood. Is it always possible to cut one of them into two pieces, so that one of the three pieces is the average length of the other two?

62

The members of a club are given membership numbers in order from 1 upwards. Ten winners are chosen at random in a prize draw, and their numbers are:

43 31 44 23 53 63 76 37 40 50

Estimate the most likely number of members in the club.

63

This is part of a table of values of $3S^2 + T^2$. Values of S are down the left-hand side and values of T along the top. Investigate any patterns you can find in this table.

(You may need to extend it to larger values of S & T)

	1	2	3	4	5	6	7	8	9	10	11	12	13
1	4	7	12	19	28	39	52	67	84	103	124	147	172
2	13	16	21	28	37	48	61	76	93	112	133	156	181
3	28	31	36	43	52	63	76	91	108	127	148	171	196
4	49	52	57	64	73	84	97	112	129	148	169	192	217
5	76	79	84	91	100	111	124	139	156	175	196	219	244
6	109	112	117	124	133	144	157	172	189	208	229	252	277
7	148	151	156	163	172	183	196	211	228	247	268	291	316

This figure shows four points, A, B, C, D: P is half way between A and B and Q is half way between C and D. X is half way between P and Q.

What middle points would you get if you started by choosing two different pairs from A and B, C and D?

A   P   B

•X

•
D

•
Q

•
C

 M

Find all the pairs of whole numbers a and b which fit this equation: $ab = 3(a-3)(b-3)$

66

Arrange two red, two green and two blue marbles so that each marble touches all four of the marbles which are a different colour from it.

67

This diagram shows how any triangle can be dissected into four identical triangles:

How many pieces are needed to dissect any quadrilateral into four identical quadrilaterals?

How many pieces for a pentagon?

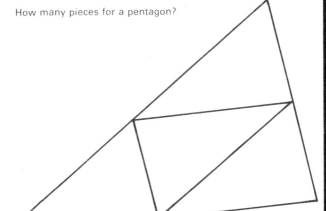

Find a rule for calculating the
areas of shapes like this, with
horizontal bases, vertical sides,
and sloping tops:

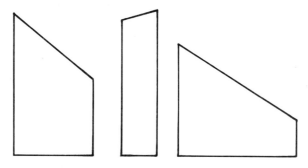

69

What is the smallest number which can be divided exactly by 5,
7, 9 and 21?

70 M

How many prime numbers are there less than 100?

71

Mary bought a small tin of peas for 24p. When she got home, Peter said, 'That's a waste of money. You can buy a tin twice as big as that for the same price at the supermarket. You've wasted 12p.'

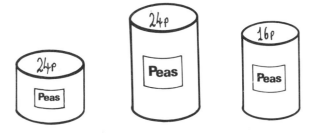

72

If, BLOB $(a + 1, b) = $ BLOB $(a, b) + b + 1$
BLOB $(a, 0) = a$
BLOB $(a, b) = $ BLOB (b, a)

calculate BLOB $(12, 5)$

73

Is it possible to divide a rectangle (any rectangle) into five smaller rectangles, each of different shape, but all of the same area?

Is it possible to divide any rectangle into seven small rectangles, under the same conditions?

74

What is the largest number of pieces which can be placed on a chessboard so that not more than two pieces are in a straight line in *any* direction, horizontally, vertically or diagonally. Even diagonals like this are *not* allowed:

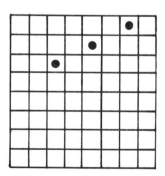

75

This map shows three small islands in the Pacific Ocean. The fishermen who live on each island are only allowed to catch fish in the part of the ocean that is nearer to their own island than it is to either of the other islands.

Is there any part of the ocean where the fish are safe, because none of the fishermen is permitted to fish there?

Investigate the problem when one of the islands is replaced by a long shore line, like this:

43

76

A is a point on one side of a quadrilateral. Is it possible to find points B, C and D on the other sides of the quadrilateral such that AB = BC = CD = DA?

Is there more than one position of A?

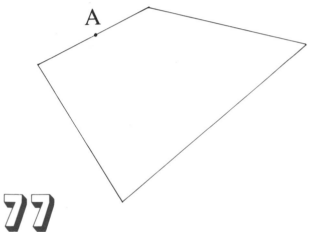

A

77

"Fourdoublehamburgersandchipsandtwocokesplease!"

How many meals fit this description?

I think of a positive number, square it, multiply by the number I first thought of, take one away, divide by one less than the number I first thought of, take away the number I first thought of, and my answer is 37.

What number did I think of?

79

A TOPOLOGICAL PROBLEM

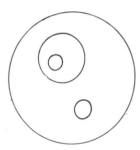

Here is one way to arrange 6 bubbles so that some of them are separate, some of them are inside each other, and some of them are inside a bubble...which is inside another bubble...and so on!

In how many different ways like this can 6 bubbles be arranged?

Do not take any account of the size of the bubbles, nor their order.

Reading down and across there are eight answers in this crossnumber indicated by the capital letters.

You are given four clues, plus the fact that no answer begins with a zero.

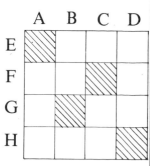

Your clues:
D = 9E
F = 9B   A = H + 91   C + G = E

If x is the sum of two integral squares, so that $x = a^2 + b^2$ where a and b are whole numbers, explain why 2x must also be the sum of two integral squares.

How can the centre of gravity of this irregular quadrilateral be found, only using a ruler?

(The centre of gravity is the point at which it would balance on a pin-point).

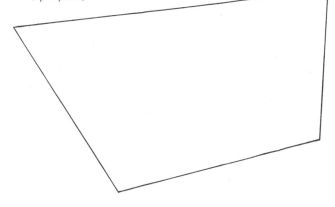

This table shows the price, energy content, and protein and fat content of three kinds of food, all per portion.

	cost (p)	energy (Kcal)	protein (gm)	fat (gm)
Cheddar cheese	20	400	25	35
Cod in batter	30	200	20	10
Chips	8	240	4	10

Roy Smith is 16 years old and needs just 3000 Kcals of energy and 75 gm of protein per day, and preferably less than 175 gm of fat. He prefers cheese to fish and has only £1.50 to spend. How many portions of each of these foods should he have for one day?

84

This diagram shows two rectangular sheets of paper over lapping so that the corner of one is just on the edge of the other.

What is special about the lengths marked a, b, c and d?

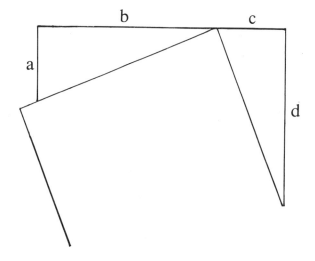

85

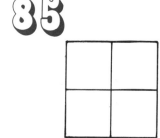

Four non-zero digits placed in these four squares will make two numbers across and two down.

If the sum of these four two-digit numbers is 67, what are they?

Find the next numbers in each of these sequences:
18 9 26 13 38 19 56 28 14 — —
1 4 2 7 5 16 14 43 41 — —
0 1 3 5 9 11 15 17 21 — —

This diagram shows a cube
with a piece cut off.
Your problem is this: can you
tell from this diagram if the
slice ABCD could be a flat
slice?

That is: could the points A, B, C
and D lie in a plane?

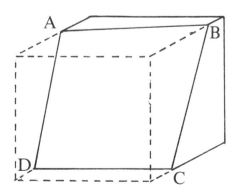

88 M

What are the prime factors of the number 22,438,769?

89

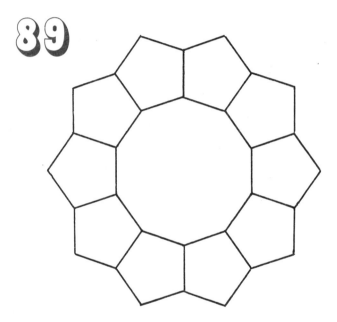

What is the simplest way to draw accurately this ring of 10 regular pentagons? (A regular pentagon has five equal sides and five equal angles).

All the answers are whole
numbers and none of the
answers begins with a zero.

Across clues
B a multiple of 320
D square root of 121
E 4 more than C down
G one ninth of A down
J one less than J down
K twice F down

Down clues
A 9 times G across
B a multiple of 7
C a prime number

F B down + C down
H same as D across
J one less than C down

A	B	C	
D		E	F
G	H	J	
K			

What is the difference between one hundred millionths, and
one hundred-millionth?

"Isn't that typical!" cried Stephen, "You wait for ages for a bus and then three turn up bunched together!"

"You know what I think," said Marion, "the buses behind ought to slow up so that they could pick up passengers who are too late to catch the bus in front — that way, people would actually get to their destinations quicker, on average."

"That can't work," replied Stephen, "if some of the buses slow down, the buses will go slower on average, and therefore the passengers must go more slowly, on average, as well."

Who is right, Stephen or Marion?

Copy the figure on the left on squared paper, cut out the pieces and rearrange them to make the figure on the right.

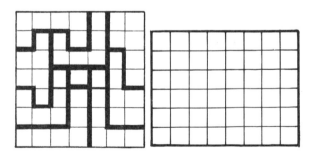

94

Three rods of lengths 10, 20 and 30 cm are all joined at one end as in the diagram. The angles between them can be changed, as you like.

How should they be arranged so that the triangle formed by their free ends has as large an area as possible?

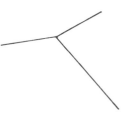

95

This is a 2 x 2 x 2 cube with one unit cube removed from one corner. What shape would you see if you looked at the damaged cube along the diagonal from the corner X which is now missing, towards the opposite corner Y?

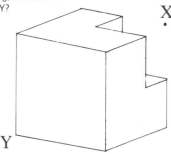

X

Y

This picture shows the appearance of a wall I noticed recently. The brickwork on the right seems to be exactly half the size of that on the left, but actually the wall zig-zags and it is just further away on the right.

Your problem is to say whether it is exactly *twice* as far away?

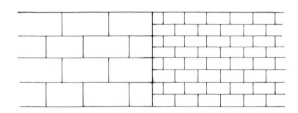

 M

Some numbers are the sum of two integral squares. That means that they are the sum of the squares of two whole numbers.

For example, $13 = 3^2 + 2^2$ and $26 = 5^2 + 1^2$

How many of the numbers from 100 to 150 are the sum of two integral squares?

How can the numbers 458, 685 and 1690 each be written as the sum of two integral squares?

Find three whole numbers, a, b and c, which will make this fraction a whole number:

$$\frac{bc + ac + ab}{a + b + c}$$

Can you find a method which will give many such solutions?

Can the whole of three-dimensional space be filled with regular tetrahedrons and regular octahedrons?

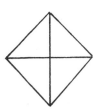

```
 74          12          12
+28         ×11         ×12
----        ----        ----
102         132         144
 03          33          45
```

This is a special kind of arithmetic. Only the numbers up to 99 are used. When you would normally have to carry into the hundreds, you carry into the units instead, as in these examples.

Your problem is: does this kind of arithmetic "work"? In other words, can you add, subtract, multiply and divide in this arithmetic without getting absurd results, or will you eventually end up by proving that 2 + 2 = 3 or some equally ridiculous answer?

This diagram shows four points such that the six distances between them are all whole numbers. Can you find 5 points with the same property? Six or more?

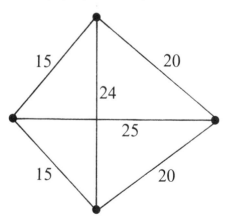

102

7 x 5 = 35	3 + 5 = 8
77 x 55 = 4235	42 + 35 = 77
777 x 555 = 431235	431 + 235 = 666

. . . .

Investigate

8 x 3 = 24	2 + 4 = 6
88 x 33 = 2904	29 + 4 = 33
888 x 333 = .295704	295 + 704 = 999

. . . .

Investigate

333 x 444 = 147852	147 + 852 = 999
333 x 777 = 258741	258 + 741 = 999
666 x 777 = 517482	517 + 482 = 999

. . . .

Investigate

The decimal for one seventh is $0.\overline{142857}$ and 142 + 857 = 999:
Is this a complete coincidence, or is there a connection with
the last patterns above?

Which is bigger: $\sqrt{80} - \sqrt{60}$ or $\sqrt{(80 - 60)}$?

104

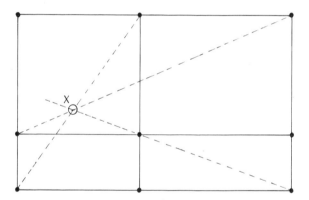

Here are 9 points arranged to form 4 rectangles, (or 9 rectangles, depending on which ones you are counting!)

As you can see, the three dotted lines in the figure all meet, rather surprisingly, at the one point, X.

How many other sets of three dotted lines can be added to this figure, so that each set also meets in a single point?

105

The instrument called a parallel rule can be used to draw a line through any point, parallel to another line already drawn. For example, it could be used to draw a line through this point L, parallel to MN. It can also be used to join two points with a straight line, but it cannot be used like an ordinary ruler to measure lengths, because the edge is not marked in any way.

L

If you are given two points X and Y, how could you use a parallel rule to find the point Z on the line joining X and Y, such that XZ = 2ZY?

106 M

Find as many points as you can, with co-ordinates (x, y), such that:
$$y^2 + x^4 + 40 < 5x^2 + 12y$$

107

"Let $S = \frac{1}{2} + \frac{1}{3} + \frac{1}{4} + \frac{1}{5} + \frac{1}{6} + \frac{1}{7} + \ldots$

Then $\frac{1}{2}S = \frac{1}{4} + \frac{1}{6} + \frac{1}{8} + \frac{1}{10} + \frac{1}{12} + \frac{1}{14} + \ldots$

So, $\frac{1}{2}S = \frac{1}{2} + \frac{1}{3} + \frac{1}{5} + \frac{1}{7} + \frac{1}{9} + \frac{1}{11} + \ldots$

Subtracting: $\frac{1}{2} + (\frac{1}{3} - \frac{1}{4}) + (\frac{1}{5} - \frac{1}{6}) + \ldots = 0$

Or: $\frac{1}{2} + \frac{1}{12} + \frac{1}{30} + \frac{1}{56} + \frac{1}{90} + \ldots = 0$"

The conclusion of this argument is nonsense; therefore, there must be an error in the argument, somewhere. Where is this error?

108

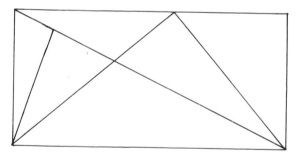

This rectangle has been divided into six pieces. How can these pieces be used to make another rectangle of different shape?

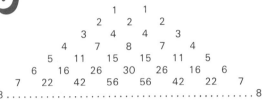

```
              1      1
          2      2      2
       3      4      4      3
    4      7      8      7      4
 5     11     15     15     11     5
6    16     26     30     26     16     6
7    22     42     56     56     42     22     7
8..........................................8
```

This triangle starts with the two outside diagonal rows 1, 2, 3, 4, 5, 6, 7, 8 . . .

The inside numbers are each the sum of the two numbers in the previous row, above right, and above left. For example, 42 = 16 + 26.

Investigate the numbers in the pattern which are exactly divisible by the primes, 7, 11, 13, . . .

Prove that if p^2 is exactly divisible by p+q, then q^2 is exactly divisible by p+q also. (p and q are both whole numbers).

Every clue in this puzzle consists of two numbers. The first number in each case is the remainder when the answer to the clue is divided by the second number.

For example: *B down* 3 : 13 means that when the answer to *B down* is divided by 13, the remainder is 3.

A	B	C	D	E
F			G	
H	J			K
L		M	N	
P			Q	

Clues across

A	0 : 5	G	40 : 94	M	20 : 99
C	83 : 166	H	3 : 7	P	10 : 336
F	7 : 11	L	6 : 11	Q	0 : 9

Clues down

A	5 : 350	D	0 : 49	K	14 : 15
B	3 : 13	E	5 : 17	L	3 : 15
C	46 : 100	J	0 : 72	N	1 : 7

You have to cut a hole in a piece of thin flat steel sheet so that a regular tetrahedron of side 10 cm will just go through the hole.

How small could the hole be, and what shape must it be if it is as small as possible?

Hints for Solutions

Ideas and suggestions which
can help, but which do not
give away the solution.

HINTS FOR SOLUTIONS

1. Put the 1 and 6 in two of the middle circles.
2. No hint.
3. Rearrange the expression p+q—pq by considering first (1—p) (1—q)
4. 'X' can force a row of four on his fourth move at the latest.
5. Systematic trial and error shows up a simple pattern, or form a quadratic equation.
6. What would happen if the two points were directly oppsite each other i.e. if the line joining them crosses the given line at right angles?
7. The roads of lengths 28 and 23 cannot possibly be needed in the solution.
8. The digit 8 only occurs twice, in 718 and 48 so these two numbers must fit together. Alternatively put all the three digit numbers in first.
9. No hint.
10. Look for bushes with 6 flowers and 0 joints; 5 flowers and 1 joint and so on.
11. Restrict your search to fractions where the numerator is 1. Because the first decimal starts 0.02 . . . the fraction must be between $\frac{1}{50}$ and $\frac{1}{33}$.
12. One idea is to start with triangles, or hexagons, (or even these 7-gons).
13. Try choosing a mixture of short lengths and very long lengths.
14. Try multiplying the expression by a suitable product of cosines.
15. Write a program to give the sum of 10 terms, then 20 terms and 50 terms. . .
16. Start by completing a table for a four-player tournament.
17. Place two rulers down to represent the two straight lines and draw some squares as an experiment.

18. How can two 'infinite' numbers possibly be compared.
19. Try a pattern with two groups of four points.
20. The shortest distance will not change if the cone is cut and flattened out.
21. Try plotting all the pairs you find on a graph.
22. The answer to each question is the same.
23. Start by joining the vertices of the pentagon to make the star.

24. Let the area of this rectangle represent the total number of errors. The errors undetected by either proof reader are represented by the area of the small rectangle in the top right-hand corner.

25. No hint.
26. 7 divides exactly into 999,999.
27. The solution has a kind of symmetry.
28. The decimal $0.xyz\overline{xyz}$ is equal to the fraction $\frac{xyz}{999}$.
   Similarly the decimal $0.wxyz\overline{wxyz}$ is equal to the fraction $\frac{wxyz}{9999}$
29. There are two solutions. In each solution two brothers must have married two sisters.
30. Cut out an actual equilateral triangle and experiment.
31. They could have come from one of the commonest solid shapes of all.

HINTS FOR SOLUTIONS

The average of two numbers is greater than the smaller and less than the greater.

If, for example, PA in this figure equals one quarter of PQ and PC equals one third of PR, then the area of PAC is one twelfth of the area of triangle PQR.

. No hint.

. Start by considering the case when the first pill is taken at 6 am.

. Make one and experiment! Move it so it has more than one axis of symmetry.

7. If the squares in each diagram are coloured black and white alternatively, how many are there of each colour? In each case try starting in the first square of the first row.

8. Compare the third line with the first line, term by term.

9. Try drawing a map.

0. There are two solutions. In one solution, the point T is on the side of the triangle.

1. A straight edge and a pair of compasses can be used to draw a line which bisects another line at right angles.

2. What is the difference between 'votes' and 'points'?

3. Calculus is not necessary. It is possible to rearrange the given expression in this form: a number — the square of an expression.

4. No hint.

45. Examine any box with one end open, as an aid to thinking!

46. No hint.

47. Start by filling in the two missing symbols in the first column, in any order.

48. From the first two pieces of information Gary is 4 years older than Alan.

49. Think about numbers which are 2 more than a multiple of 6, or 3 or 4 more . . .

50. Try it and see.

51. If figures are similar, their areas are in the ratio of the squares of their sides.

52. No hint.

53. Try some numbers and see what happens. Each problem gives its own result, which will always be the same.

54. Look at the relationship between the first and second number in each pair of brackets.

55. Use tracing paper.

56. No hint.

57. A 1/8 chance that 3 people will enter means that on average 3/8ths of a person will enter!

58. No hint.

59. One of the possible cross-sections of a tetrahedron is a square.

60. Measure possible routes and calculate the times.

61. The average of two numbers is one half of their sum.

62. Think about the significance of the largest number.

63. There are many different kinds of patterns to be discovered. One type appears when you look only at the units digits, for example.

HINTS FOR SOLUTIONS

64. Think of the original points as equal heavy weights, and P as the point where the top two weights would balance.
65. There are two pairs of two solutions.
66. Make the marbles of any two colours form a square.
67. First divide the quadrilateral into triangles.
68. Try rearranging the tops, to make them flat.
69. What is the smallest number which can be divided by 5 and 7?
70. Exclude all numbers which are multiples of 2, then multiples of 3, etc. At the end the prime numbers are left.
71. No hint.
72. Work backwards *from* BLOB (12, 5).
73. No hint.
74. No hint.
75. Think about it from the point of view of a fish.
76. Note that the question asks you to show that B, C and D exist. To actually construct them would be much more difficult. Choose a point to start with and a length for AB, BC, and CD. If DA is not the same length, make an adjustment.
77. There are 3. What are they?
78. Call the number thought of x, and solve the algebraic equation, or use trial and error.
79. Show first that 4 bubbles can be arranged in 9 ways and 5 bubbles in 20 ways. Then carry on.
80. "D" must start with a "9".
81. You may get a hint by considering how 34 is the sum of two squares, and comparing it with $17 = 4^2 + 1^2$
82. Join both diagonals. Remember that you can use a ruler for measuring.

83. The "best" answer will not necessarily satisfy all the conditions exactly. Look for an answer which is as close as possible to what is required.
84. Try it and see.
85. No hint.
86. First sequence — there is a difference between odd and even; second — the numbers go in pairs; third — prime numbers!
87. Consider where pairs of straight lines ought to meet each other — and where.
88. a is a factor of x if the integer part of
$$\frac{x}{a} \text{ is equal to } \underline{x}. \text{ Use this in a program.}$$
$$ a$$
89. Start by marking 10 points at equal intervals round a circle.
90. Start with D Across.
91. No hint.
92. No hint.
93. There is a trick somewhere, because the left-hand figure is 7 x 7 (area 49) and the right-hand figure is only 6 x 8 (area 48).
94. Imagine two of the rods are fixed in position and the third is swinging round. At what position will it make the area a maximum?
95. Make a model using sugar cubes.
96. The apparent size of an object depends on the angle made by its edges and the observer's eye.
97. Using the idea of nested loops a computer will print all the sums of squares in seconds, or use the ideas in problem 81.
98. bc + ac + ab = (a + b + c) (b + c) — (b² + c² + bc).
99. A regular tetrahedron can be inscribed in a cube.
100. The number 99 is important. Try some different types of sums in this arithmetic.

HINTS FOR SOLUTIONS

101. For five points — look where the vertical and horizontal lines on the diagram intersect.
102. 147852 is exactly divisible by 999.
103. No hint.
104. Other points can be found inside the diagram, but there are also two points outside the original figure where sets of three lines meet.
105. Parallelograms are necessary. First draw one so X and Y are at opposite corners.
106. There are some points near to $(1\frac{1}{2}, 6)$.
107. What is the sum of $\frac{1}{2} + \frac{1}{3} + \frac{1}{4} + \frac{1}{5} + \ldots?$ (If it has a sum?)
108. Copy the diagram on to thin card. Cut it out and see.
109. Continue the triangle to at least the row starting with 13. Ring the numbers which are divisible by the primes 7, 11, 13 in different colours. Can you see a pattern?
110. If two numbers are each divisible by the same other number, then so are their sum and their difference.
111. A across ends in 0 or 5 so B down begins with a 5.
112. Make a tetrahedron and consider at what angle it must be held.

 If at first you don't succeed, try, try again.
(W.E. Hickson)

If at first you don't succeed, try, try again.
Then quit. No point in being a damn fool about it.
(W.C. Fields)

SOLUTIONS

The solutions are printed upside-down
to discourage all except the truly desperate.
See the quotations opposite.

104. There are five more sets of three lines with the labelling of this figure. They are the meeting points of:

A — B — C

D — E — F

G — H — I

BI, AF, GE; AH, CE, DI; CH, AE, FG; BD, CG, FH; BF, AI, DH.

105. The first figure shows how, by using the parallel rule to draw two pairs of parallel lines through A and B, it is possible to find the midpoint E of AB by joining the two new vertices C and D. In the second diagram, a parallelogram XVYU has been drawn in the same way, and W is the midpoint of XV, found by the method of the first figure.
Join W to U and let WU cross XY at Z. Then XZ = ½ ZY.

106. All the points which satisfy the inequality are inside two small ovals. One oval is in the first quadrant and its ends are at (1, 6) and (2, 6). The second oval is the reflection of the first in the y-axis.

107. The series in the first line does not have a finite sum. If you add enough terms you can make it as large as you please!
Therefore it is a mistake to call its 'sum' S, and you certainly cannot start working out ½ S.

108. There are two different solutions which may be found with the cut-out pieces.

109. If you ring the numbers which are divisible by the primes 7, 11, 13, . . . in different colours, you will find patterns of triangles, each triangle 'upsidedown' compared with the original triangle.

110. $p^2 - q^2$ is always divisible by $p + q$ because $p^2 - q^2 = (p-q)(p+q)$. If p^2 is also divisible by $p+q$ then so is $p^2 - (p^2 - q^2) = q^2$.

111. Reading across from top to bottom one solution is: 35 — 249/557 — 40/51411/94 — 416/346 — 54.
Problem
Find another value for H across.

112. The first figure shows a top view of a tetrahedron: its shadow is a square. The second figure shows the shape of the smallest hole. Drop the tetrahedron in, and when it is half way through, twist it through 90° and it will fall out the other side.

The last expression can very easily be made into a whole number, because the term 'a' only occurs in one position. Therefore, simply choose b and c to be any numbers you like, and choose 'a' to make a + b + c equal to one of the factors of $b^2 + c^2 + bc$.

99. The first figure shows how a regular tetrahedron can be constructed in a cube. In the second diagram four tetrahedrons have been constructed in four adjacent cubes. The hole created is one half of an octahedron. If this construction is repeated throughout a solid tesselation of cubes, then space will be filled with regular tetrahedrons and regular octahedrons.

100. Yes, it does work. It is actually an example of 'clock arithmetic' in which you count round a clock back to where you started from — except in this case you are counting all the way to 99 before returning to 1

101. The simplest fifth point is the point E where the two lines cross, which is 9 and 16 units from A and C respectively. The simplest sixth and seventh points are found by reflecting the whole figure in the line BD.

There are other figures with the same property, and containing more points.

102. Let pqr be a three digit number, then pqr + 1000 (999 — pqr) = 999 (1000 — pqr). The first expression is the six digit number whose digits are pqr in the hundreds, tens and units, and (999 — pqr) in the first three places. In other words it is a number whose digits add up to 999 when split into two groups of three. The second expression shows that it will always be a multiple of 999. The opposite conclusion is also true — any multiple of 999 makes a six digit number with this property. Because $0.142857 = \frac{1}{7}$, $142857 = 999,999 \div 7$ and therefore 142557 is a multiple of 999. So naturally $142 + 857 = 999$.

103. $\sqrt{(80 — 60)}$ is bigger.

89. Draw a circle and then ten radii at intervals of 36°, extending each of them outside the circle. Join the ten points on the circumference to make a regular decagon. Then use compasses set to the side of the decagon to construct the pentagons.

90. Reading across from top to bottom, the solution is 8 — 960/11 — 71/91 — 65/316 — 8.

91.
$$\frac{100}{1,000,000} - \frac{1}{100,000,000} = \frac{9,999}{100,000,000}$$

92. Marion is almost always right. The time taken to get to your destination is equal to the time spent on the bus plus the time spent waiting for the bus to arrive. If buses bunch together, so that one bus every 10 minutes becomes two buses together every twenty minutes you will almost certainly lose more time by waiting longer, on average, than you will save from some buses going a little faster.

93. If the figure on the left, which seems to have area of 49 units, will fit into the right-hand figure whose area is 48 units, then the middle single square on the left must be a hole. The diagram shows one way to fit the remaining eight pieces into the rectangle.

Problem
How many other ways can you find?

94. Imagine first that two of the rods, say OB and OC are fixed. Then OA can be rotated until it is perpendicular to BC and the area of ABC is as large as possible. This suggests that the maximum area of ABC when all the rods can be adjusted will be when AO, BO and CO are all at right angles to their opposite sides. There is one such position and it is indeed the maximum.
Problem
What is the value of the maximum area?

95.

96. Yes, they are.

97. 18. $458 = 13^2 + 17^2$
$685 = 3^2 + 26^2 = 18^2 + 19^2$
$1690 = 13^2 + 39^2 = 27^2 + 31^2$

98.
$$\frac{bc + ac + ab}{a + b + c}$$

$$= (b + c) - \frac{(b^2 + c^2 + bc)}{a + b + c}$$

SNOITUL OS

equal x also, and in fact it is a little less. So by choosing x a little less, B, C and D will retreat anticlockwise round the quadrilateral and the distance DA will be slightly increased. In this way it is clear that by choosing different points for A, there are many rhombuses which can be inscribed in the original quadrilateral.

77. (Four double hamburgers) and chips and two cokes.
(Four (double hamburgers and chips)) and two cokes
Four (double hamburgers and chips and two cokes)

78. 6.

79. 48. Can you see why this is really the same problem as number 10?

80. A = 999, B = 10, C = 58, D = 981, E = 109, F = 90, G = 51, H = 908.

81. If $x = a^2 + b^2$
then $2x = 2a^2 + 2b^2$
$= (a^2 - 2ab + b^2) + (a^2 + 2ab + b^2)$
$= (a - b)^2 + (a + b)^2$

82. Find the centres of gravity of the two triangles on either side of one of the diagonals and join them with a straight line. Then do the same for the triangles on either side of the other diagonal. The centre of gravity is where these two lines meet.

83. There is not one single exact solution. One solution which meets most of the conditions is 3 portions of cheese, 1 of cod and 7 portions of chips. He then eats too much fat.

84. ad = bc (because the two triangles are similar in shape).

85. The numbers, reading across, are 12 and 17.
Problem
Can you solve the same problem when the sum is 65, 66, 68, 69 and 70?

86. 1st sequence: the rule is, if the number is even, halve it, if it is odd, multiply by 3 and subtract 1. The next two terms are 7 and 20.
2nd sequence: the rule is, the third, fifth, seventh, . . . numbers in the sequence are each 2 less than the previous number; the second, fourth, sixth, . . . numbers are 3 times the previous number, plus 1. The next two terms are 124, 122.
3rd sequence: 2 has been taken from each of the prime numbers 2, 3, 5, 7, 11, 13, 17, 19, 23, . . .The next two terms are 27, 29.

87. The four points where AB meets ab, CD meets cd, AD meets ad and BC meets bc, all lie in the plane abcd and also in the plane ABCD (if it is a plane).

Therefore, they should lie in the line where these two planes meet. Using a piece of tracing paper to mark the four meeting points, they do *not* lie on a straight line and so ABCD cannot possibly be a flat slice.
This method would not work if the planes were parallel, but in this case it is obvious from the diagram that they are not.

88. 53, 67, 71 and 89.

SNOITUOS

but, of course, this number is impossible to prove..

63. No solution given.

64. No matter how you split the four points into two pairs in order to find P and Q, the middle point of P and Q, X, will always be the same.

65. The solutions are a = −9, 0, 3, 4, 5, 6, 9, 18 and the matching values of b are b = 4, 3, 0, −9, 18, 9, 6, 5.

66. Arrange them at the vertices of a regular octahedron as in this figure.

67. Six pieces for the quadrilateral. Divide the quadrilateral into two triangles by drawing a diagonal and then divide each triangle into four pieces as in the problem. Total — eight pieces, but two pairs of pieces do not actually need to be separated.

A pentagon can be dissected by drawing a diagonal which divides it into a triangle and a quadrilateral, but again some of the pieces do not need to be separated, so the minimum number of pieces needed is only 8.

68. Multiply the base by the *average* of the two sides at right-angles to the base.

69. 5 × 7 × 3 × 3 = 315, so the smallest number is 315.

70. 25.

71. They are both right in their own way. If Mary can only make use of the peas in a small tin, then she is right, and she has only wasted 8p

by going to the nearest shop. Peter would only be right if they could use up a large quantity of peas.

72. BLOB (12, 5) = BLOB (5, 12) = 77
Problem
Can you calculate BLOB (−12, 5) and BLOB (12, −5)? What happens when you try to calculate BLOB (−12, −5)?

73. No, at least two of the rectangles must be the same shape, in each case.

74. The largest possible number is 16, so that there are two pieces in every row and every column. Here is one way to achieve this, reading across from top to bottom. (P stands for piece; the numbers are the numbers of spaces between pieces or the edge of the board).
P6P/2P2P2/1P4P1/3PP3/1P4P1/P6P/3PP3/2P2P2.

75. If a fish asks itself if there is one of these islands which is nearer than any other the answer must always be yes. Nowhere is therefore safe. Certain points will be equidistant from two or even three islands, but points are not large enough for a fish to hide in!

76. In the figure the point A was chosen to start with, together with the distance x. B, C and D were marked so that AB, BC and CD all equal x. Naturally DA cannot be expected to

51. OB, is twice as long as OA₁. Therefore OB₁ B₂ is 4 times the area of OA A₂. So the difference between them A₁ B₁ B₂ A₂ is three times the area of OA₁ A₂. Similarly B₁ C₁ C₂ B₂ is five times the area of OA₁ A₂. Therefore B₁ D₁ D₂ B₂ = 3 x OB₁ B₂ and so on.

52. 18.

53. In the first problem you can choose any number at all for the first square you choose, and on calculating the remaining squares, they will fit perfectly.
On the other hand, no solution is possible for the second problem. The sum of the four numbers, added in rows is 12 + 29 = 41, but the sum added in columns is apparently 24 + 15 = 39. This is a contradiction and so a solution is impossible.
It is impossible to invent a problem of the same kind which has only *one* solution.

54. (7, 12) and (5, 10) are the points which do not lie on the straight line. For any other pair of points the differences between the second numbers in each pair are double the differences between the first numbers, which means that if the graph were to be drawn, its gradient would be 2.
For example, 17 − 11 = 6 and 9 − 6 = 3.

55. Trace the rectangle onto tracing paper and cut it out. The short side of the rectangle can be divided into 4 by folding in half, then in half again. The long side can be divided into 6 by folding in thirds and then into halves. The divisions can then be transferred back to the original diagram.

56. 99,999.

57. The average number of customers expected to arrive in 1 minute is
$1 \times \frac{1}{2} + 2 \times \frac{1}{4} + 3 \times \frac{1}{8} + \ldots$
This series sums to 2, so on average 2 people will enter each minute, or 4 people will enter in the two minutes it takes to serve one customer. So four cashiers should be kept busy.

58. **No, every straight line through X will be divided 2 : 1 except the unique line through X which is parallel to both horizontal lines.**

59. No. Although one of the possible cross-sections of a tetrahedron is a square, it can only be pushed through the square hole which it will just fit, by squashing and distorting it — which presumably is not possible if it is made of *hard* rubber.

60. He should go North to leave the desert as soon as possible and then skirt the edge until there is a clear straight line to Z.

61. The average of two numbers is one third of the sum of the numbers *and* the average itself. Therefore, to solve the problem it is only necessary to cut off from one piece of wood a length equal to one third of the total length of the two pieces — which is certainly possible.

62. **There must be 76 members as this is the highest number drawn. From the distribution of the numbers one might expect about 90 members,**

SOLUTIONS

$1/2 = 1/3 + 1/9 + 1/27 + 1/81 + \ldots$ which is in fact the case.

39. In the first case, yes, he has enough information to draw a map complete with scale. In the second case he has enough information to draw the map in the correct proportions, provided there were at least three landmarks measured. However, since no distances were measured, no scale can be marked on the map.

40. In the simplest solution with the given lengths, the point T is on the side of the equilateral triangle, whose edges are of length 8. There is another solution in which T is outside the triangle, whose edges are of length $\sqrt{19}$.

41. Mark three points A, B, C on the circumference. The perpendicular bisectors of AB and BC meet at the centre of the circle.

42. The figures may look suspicious because the points awarded to each sportsman are closer together than the votes. However, this can easily be explained. For example, it might be that the correspondents who did not vote Botham first, did not give him points either for their second or third choices, while those who did vote for Botham gave points to Coe and Davis as their second and third choices.

43. The expression has the value 24 when t = 1, 2, 3 or 4. However, its value is less than 24 between 2 and 3, and greater than 24 between 1 and 2, and between 3 and 4. (It is zero when t is 0 or 5)
The maximum value is 25 when t = 1.38 or t = 3.62.
Problem
What is its minimum value?

44. One solution is

1	13	4	16
8	12	5	9
14	2	15	3
11	7	10	6

Problem
Can you find at least one more solution?

45. The diagonal width of the inside block must not be greater than 10 cm, and the largest block is a cube whose edges are approximately 7.07 cm.

46. No solution.

47. Yes, it is always possible to complete a Latin square. One of the remaining rows in the problem is

Π	+	ß	I	o

48. Alan is 12, two years younger than Caroline. Gary is 16, four years older than Alan. Mary is 13.

49. Numbers which are 2 or 4 more than a multiple of 6 are bound to be even, because all multiples of 6 are even, and so they cannot be prime. Any number which is 3 more than a multiple of six will be divisible by 3, because all multiples of 6 are divisible by 3.
So that only leaves 1 more or 1 less than a multiple of 6 for the prime numbers. The two exceptions are 2 and 3.

50. After six movements, two in each direction, you will always get back to the point where you started.
Problem
Does the same thing happen if four directions are chosen?

SOLUTIONS

28. 41. As a fraction, the percentage given is

$\frac{7046}{11111}$ which cancels downs to $\frac{26}{41}$.

So the smallest number of people who could have been asked the question is 41, of whom 26 replied 'yes'.

29. There are two solutions.
(1) Anita is Mike's niece.
The family tree is:—

```
        Sally           Gregory
      ┌──────┐        ┌────────┐
Y =Mike     John = X    Y = Mike
  |                |
Peter            Anita
```

(2) Anita is Mike's daughter.
The family tree is:—

```
        Sally           Gregory
      ┌──────┐        ┌────────┐
Y = Mike    John = X    Y = Mike
  |                |
Anita            Peter
```

30. The equilateral triangle will be as large as possible when the four nearest dots touch its sides, like this:

The side of the triangle will then be $1 + \frac{2}{\sqrt{3}}$ times the side of the square.

31. They could have been cut from a cube, or from many cuboids (rectangular boxes).

32. $\frac{7}{17} = \frac{84}{204}$ and $\frac{5}{12} = \frac{85}{204}$ so one fraction in between is $\frac{84\frac{1}{2}}{204}$ or $\frac{169}{408}$.

33. This is one possible solution. There are many others.

34. No. According to the first two equations C must be 2 more than A, not 1 more as the last equation states.

35. 12.

36. The knot can be moved into this symmetrical formation. It now has three axes of symmetry.

37. In the first figure it is possible to start anywhere you choose and visit every square once before returning to the square you started from.
If the second figure is coloured black and white alternately, like a chess board, then there will be three more squares of one colour than the other. Since a knight move takes a piece from a black square to a white square, or *vice versa*, it is impossible to visit all the squares. At least two must be omitted.
Problem
Try the same problem using a grid with four squares in the top row, six in the second, etc.

38. Each term in the third line is exactly one third of the corresponding term in the first line, although the two sums are apparently equal to each other.
This suggests that each sum must be zero, and therefore that

SNOITULOS

14. $\frac{1}{8}$.
15. 2, 3.
16.

	A	B	C	D	E	F	G	H
A		1	2	3	4	5	6	7
B	1		3	2	7	4	5	6
C	2	3		1	6	7	4	5
D	3	2	1		5	6	7	4
E	4	7	6	5		1	2	3
F	5	4	7	6	1		3	2
G	6	5	4	7	2	3		1
H	7	6	5	4	3	2	1	

Problem
In how many different ways can the table be completed?

17. S and T both move along straight lines.

18. Neither. A mathematician would say that they have the same number of numbers each, because they can be matched exactly: each number in the first sequence can be matched against its own square in the second sequence.

19. Yes, in many different ways. Here is a simple way to arrange eight points.

    •
  •   •
  •   •

  •   •
         •

Problem
Can 9 points be marked so it is *not* possible to draw a convex pentagon?

20. The shortest distance is 26.46 cm.

21. (2, 7), (5, 5), (8, 3) and (11, 1) are the only pairs of positive whole numbers which fit. An infinite number of pairs of fractions will fit it, including the average of any of the pairs above. For example, the average of (5, 5) and (8, 3) is (6½, 4) which fits. If all the pairs are plotted on a graph, they will lie on a straight line.

22. 5 roads is the only possible number. If there were fewer it would be impossible to join all the towns. If there were more, it would be possible to make some journeys in more than one way.

23. The five pieces of the pentagon which are not needed for the first pentagon star have each been divided into two parts, A and B. The five A pieces will make the arms of a second pentagon star, while the five B pieces are more than sufficient to make the centre of the second star.

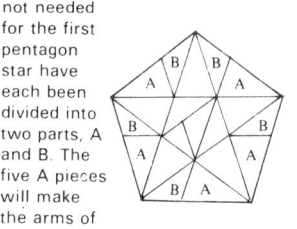

24. The best estimate is 100.8 errors — say 101.

25. The second statement only.

26. Reading across, from top to bottom, the completed square is:
142857/714285/571428/857142/285714/428571.

27. The required line segment is the one which is *bisected* by P.

SOLUTIONS

1. The 6 and the 1 should be placed in two of the middle circles. The 5 and the 2 can be placed three ways.

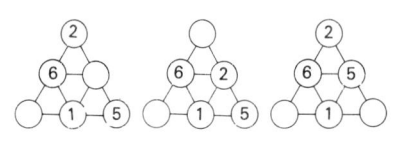

The 3 and 4 may be placed either way round.
The differences add up to 26.

2. 177768889, 277755556.
   19. The sequence 19^2, 199^2, 1999^2... has the same pattern.

3. If p and q are between 0 and 1, so are (l—p) and (l—q), and therefore so are (l—p) (l-q) and l — (l—p) (l-q) which equals p+q — pq.

4. Crosses moves: Far right-hand corner of the bottom layer, followed by near left hand corner of top layer, and then the nearest-but-one square in the left-hand column of the top layer. Noughts moves are forced each time.

5. 5

6. No. The exceptions are when the points are directly opposite each other (i.e. a line joining them would cross the given line at right angles), but different distances from the line.

7. Our shortest route goes like this:
   14 — 26 — 20 — 10 — 11 — 12 — 25 — 18 — 13 — 9 — 19. Total distance travelled, 177. (Because the route ends where it started, he can choose to start from any town).
   Problem
   Which is the shortest route if he has to travel along each road at least once to call on customers as well as visit each town?

8. Reading across from top to bottom:
   16 — 12 — 62/3 — 32 — 79 — 7/335 — 247/299 — 739/5 — 40 — 11 — 0/21˙ — 48 — 53
   There are other slightly different solutions.

9. (N + 1) (N — 2) always equals N^2 — N — 2.

10. With 6 flowers and 0 joints there is 1 bush
    with 5 flowers and 1 joint there are 5 bushes
    with 4 flowers and 2 joints there are 14 bushes
    with 3 flowers and 3 joints there are 18 bushes
    with 2 flowers and 4 joints there are 9 bushes
    with 1 flower and 5 joints there is 1 bush.
    There are 48 different bushes.

11. $\frac{1}{49}$ and $\frac{1}{97}$.

12. Here is one simple way to turn a pattern of equilateral triangles into identical 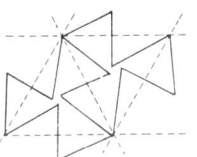 9-sided polygons by breaking each side into three parts.

13. Yes, in many ways. For example, make a triangle with the 4, 5, 6 pieces and add the 7, 8 pieces to make a second triangle with the 6. Then adjust the angle between the triangles until the 9 piece will fit. Choose two small numbers and four large numbers and it will be impossible to make any tetrahedron, because the three smallest numbers will not make a triangle e.g. 1, 2, 10, 11, 12, 13.

SOLUTIONS

SOLUTIONS
AND SOME
FURTHER PROBLEMS
& INVESTIGATIONS